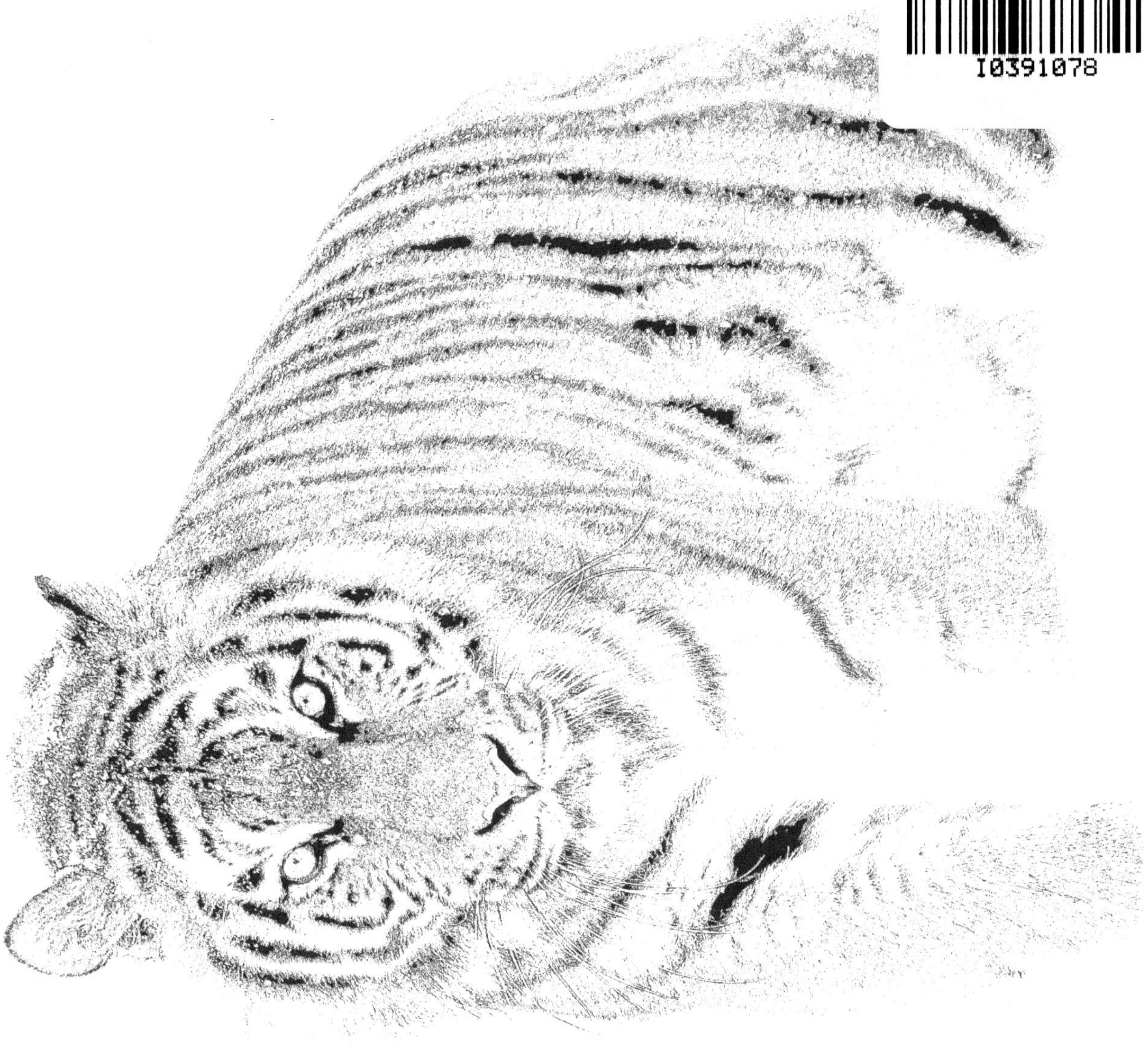

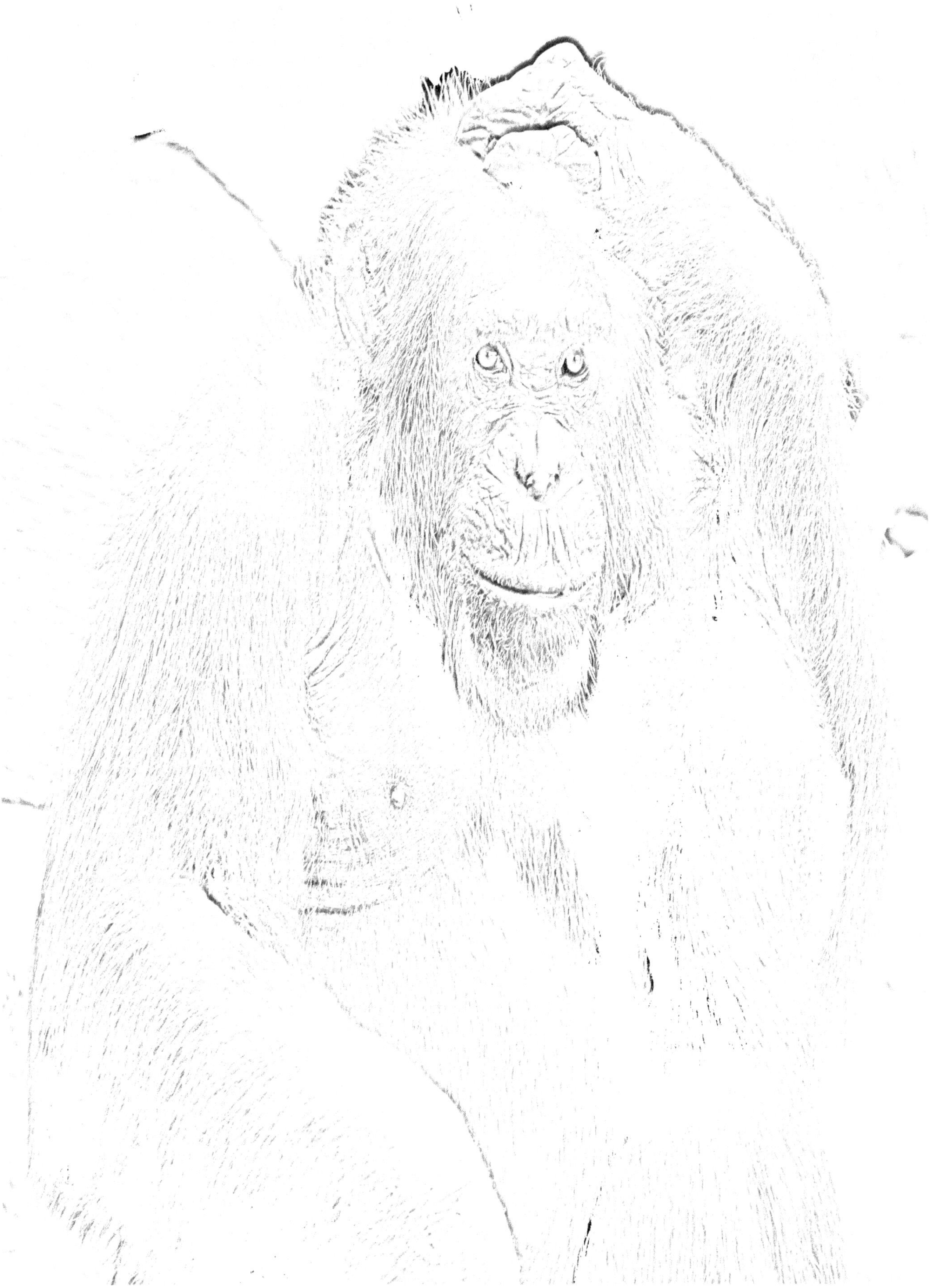

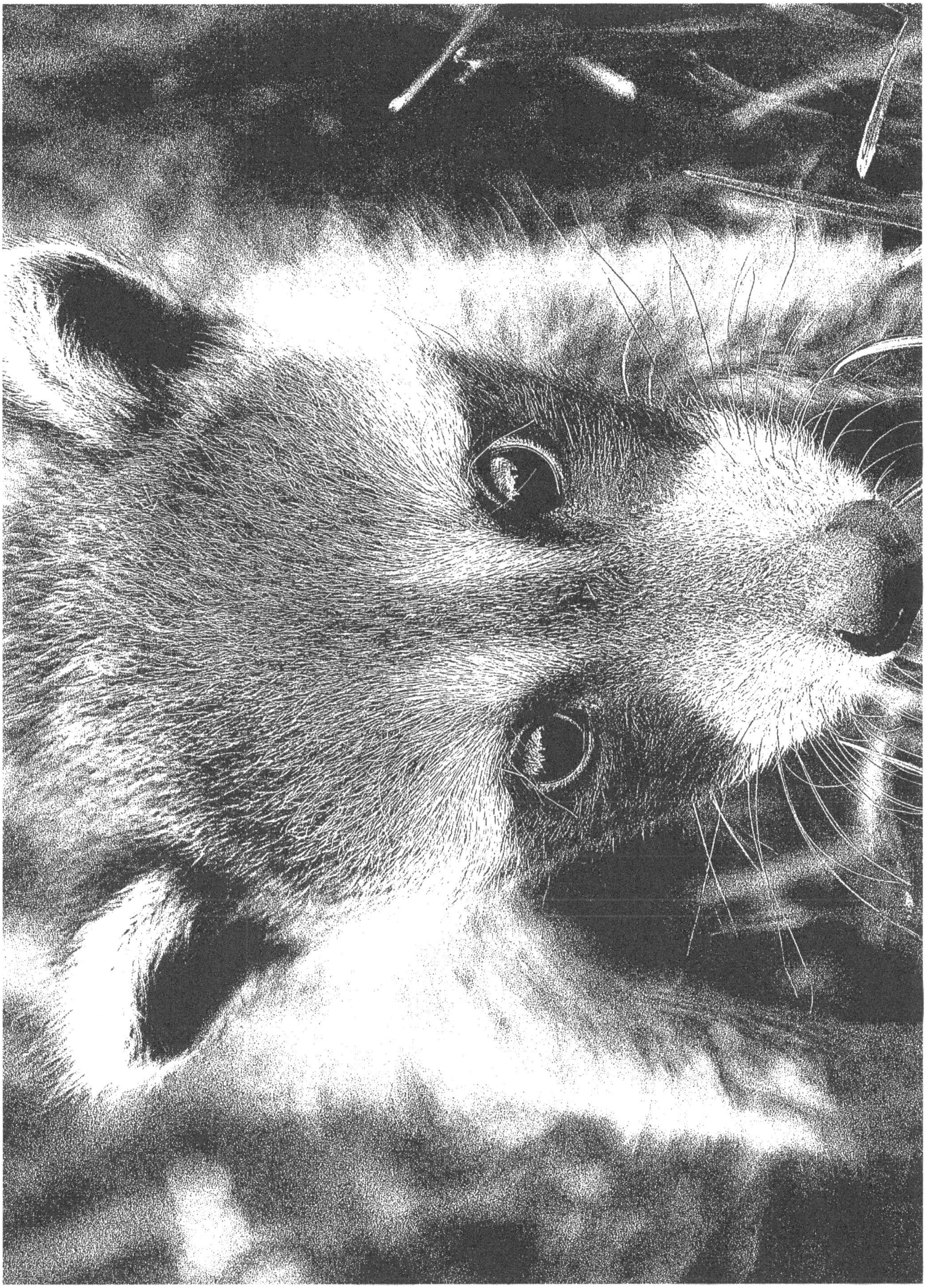

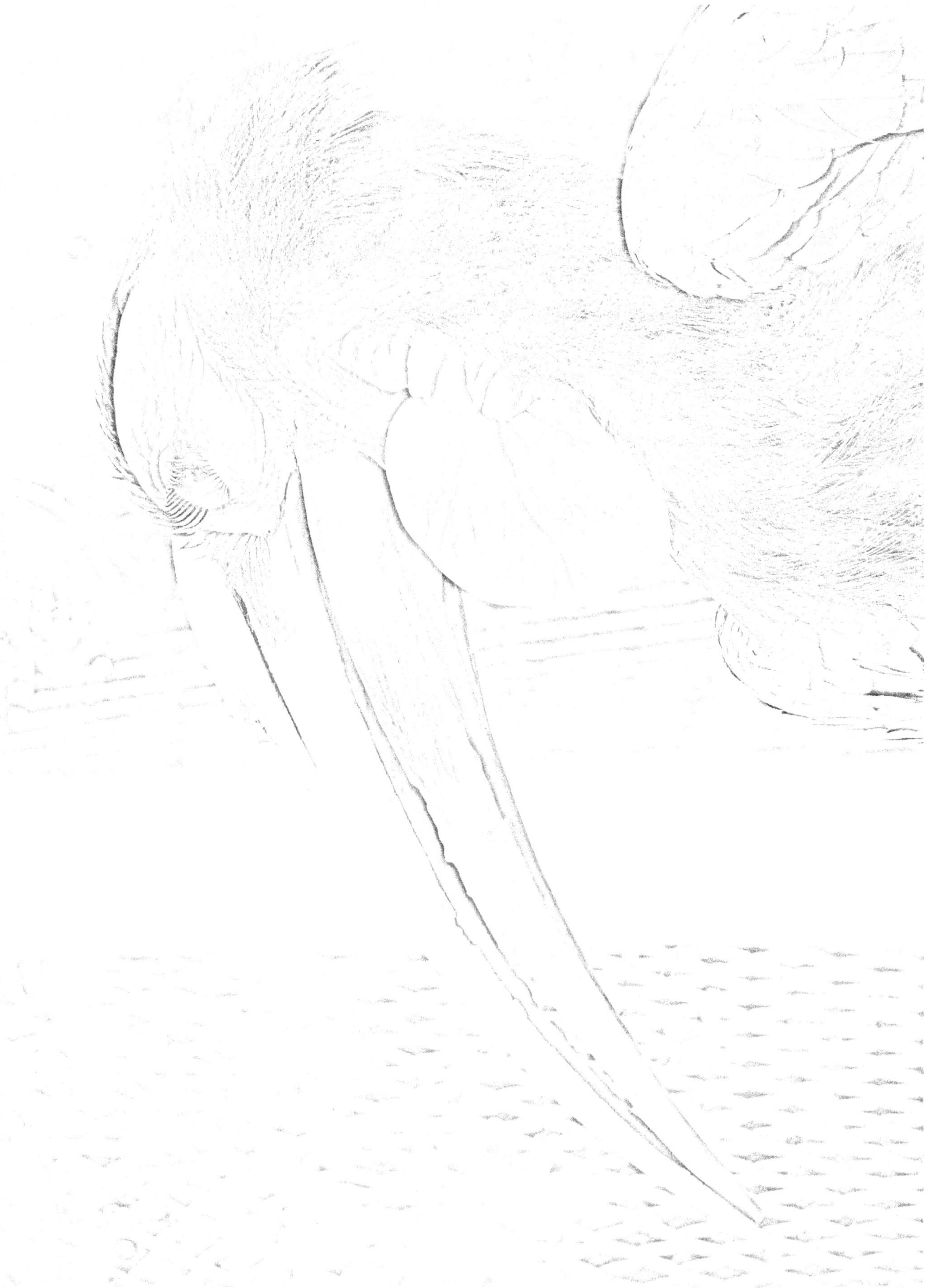

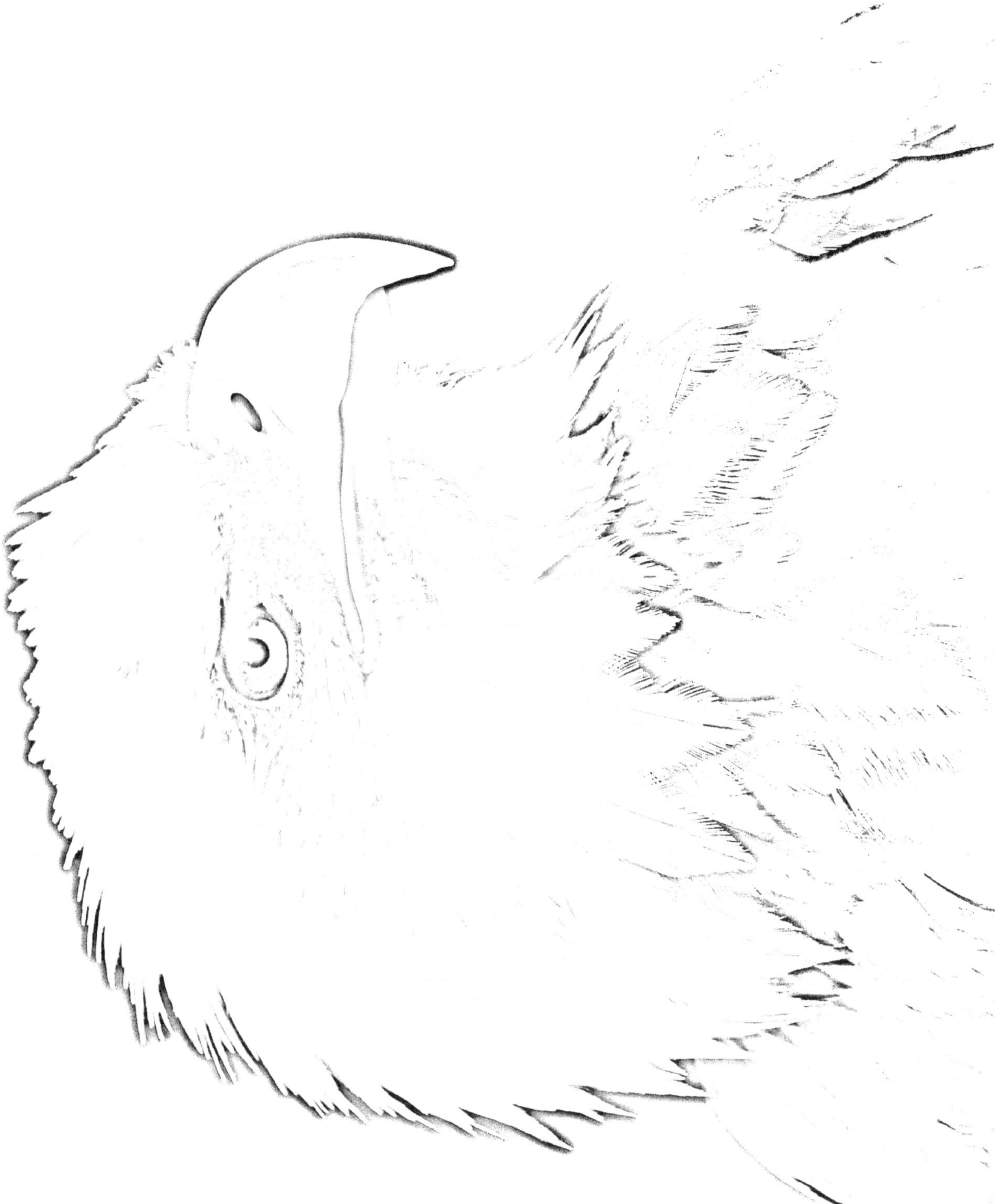

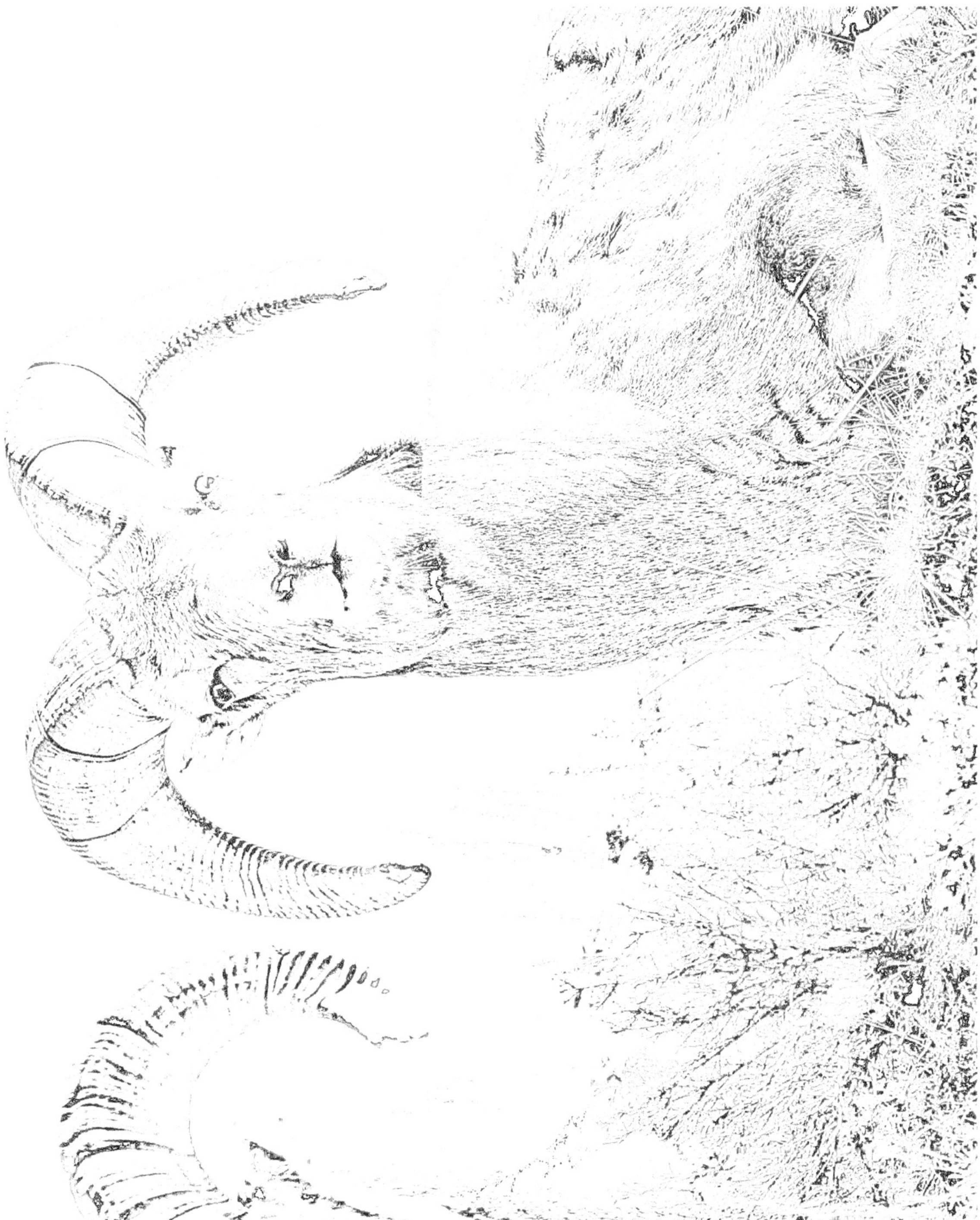

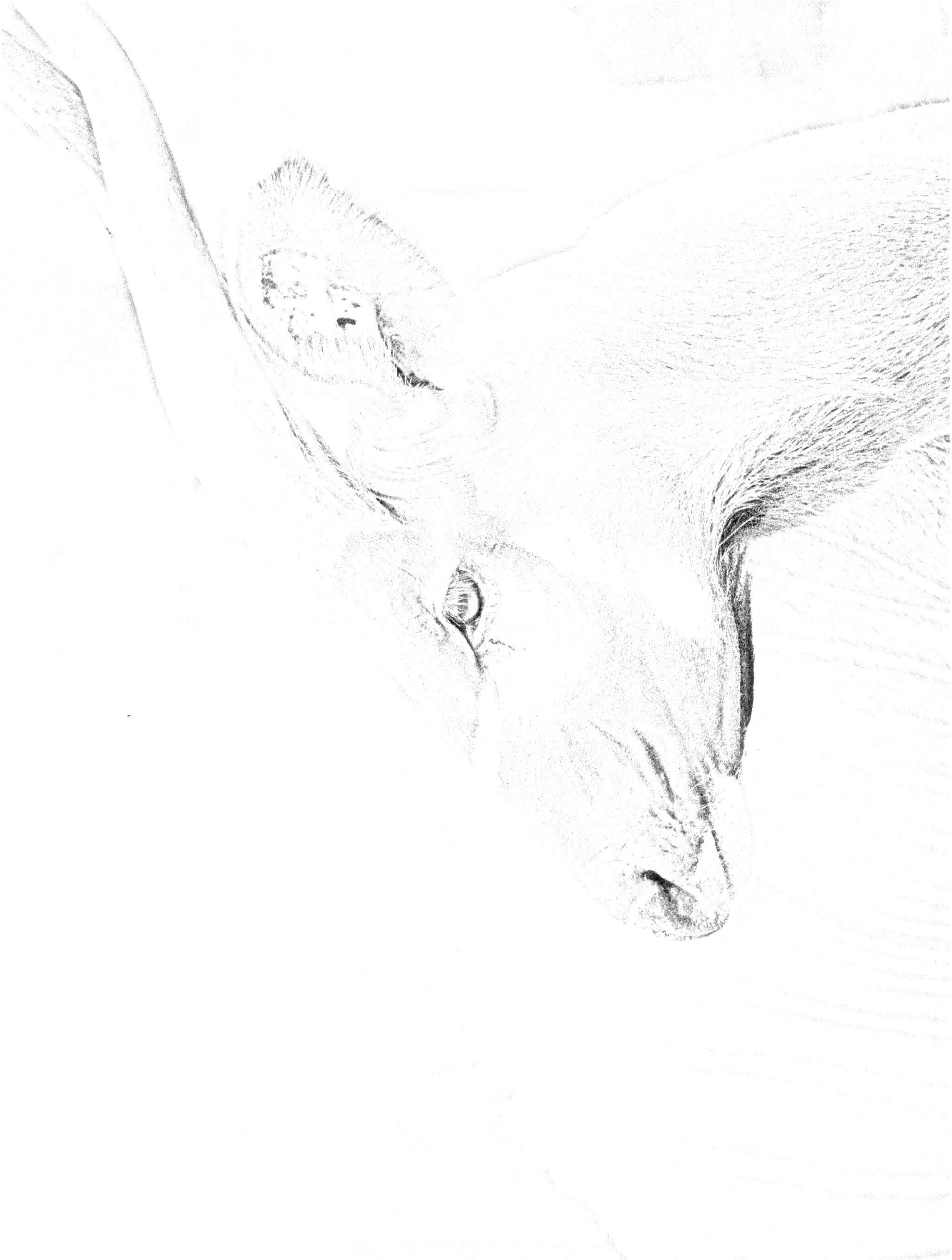

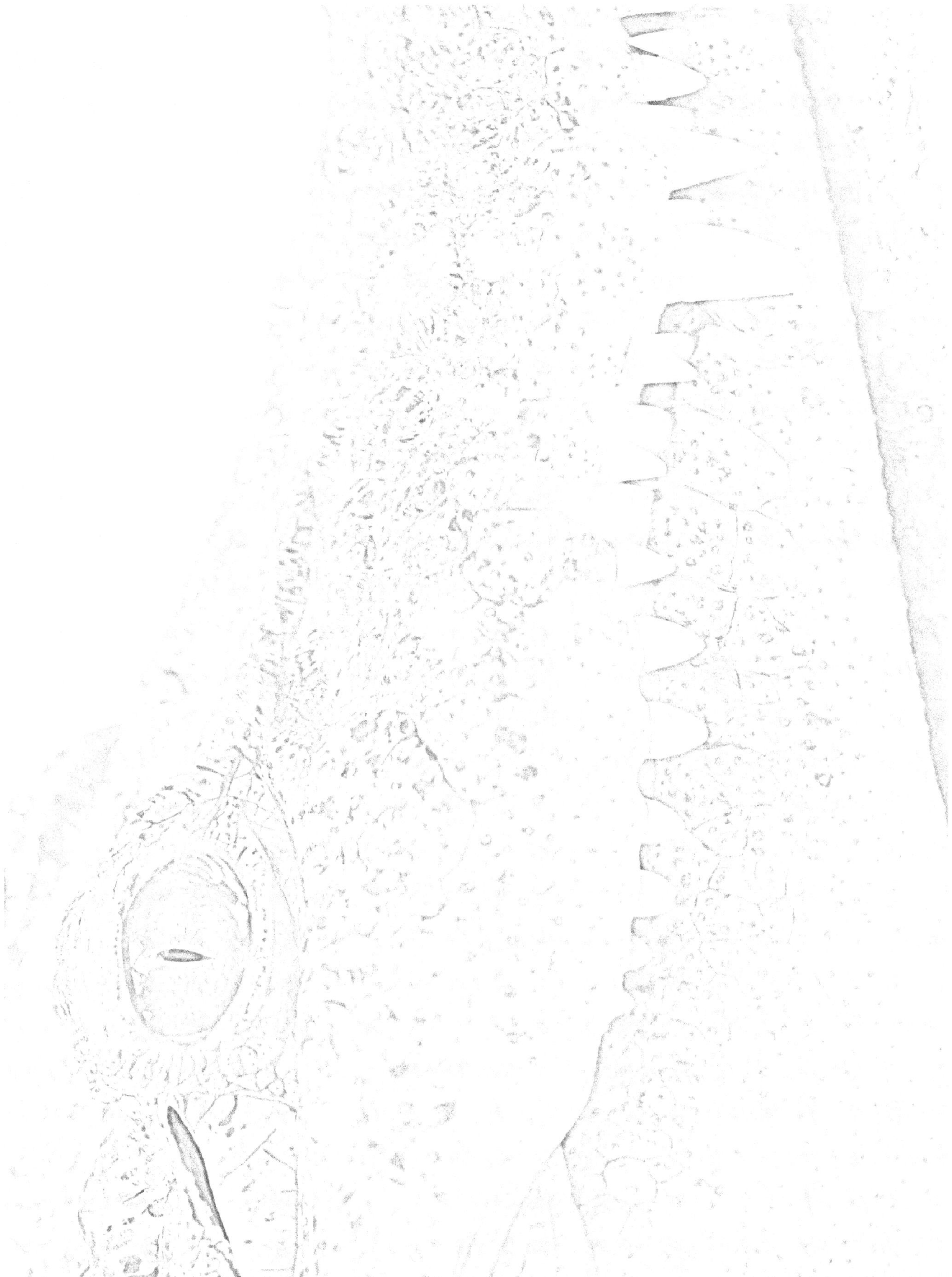

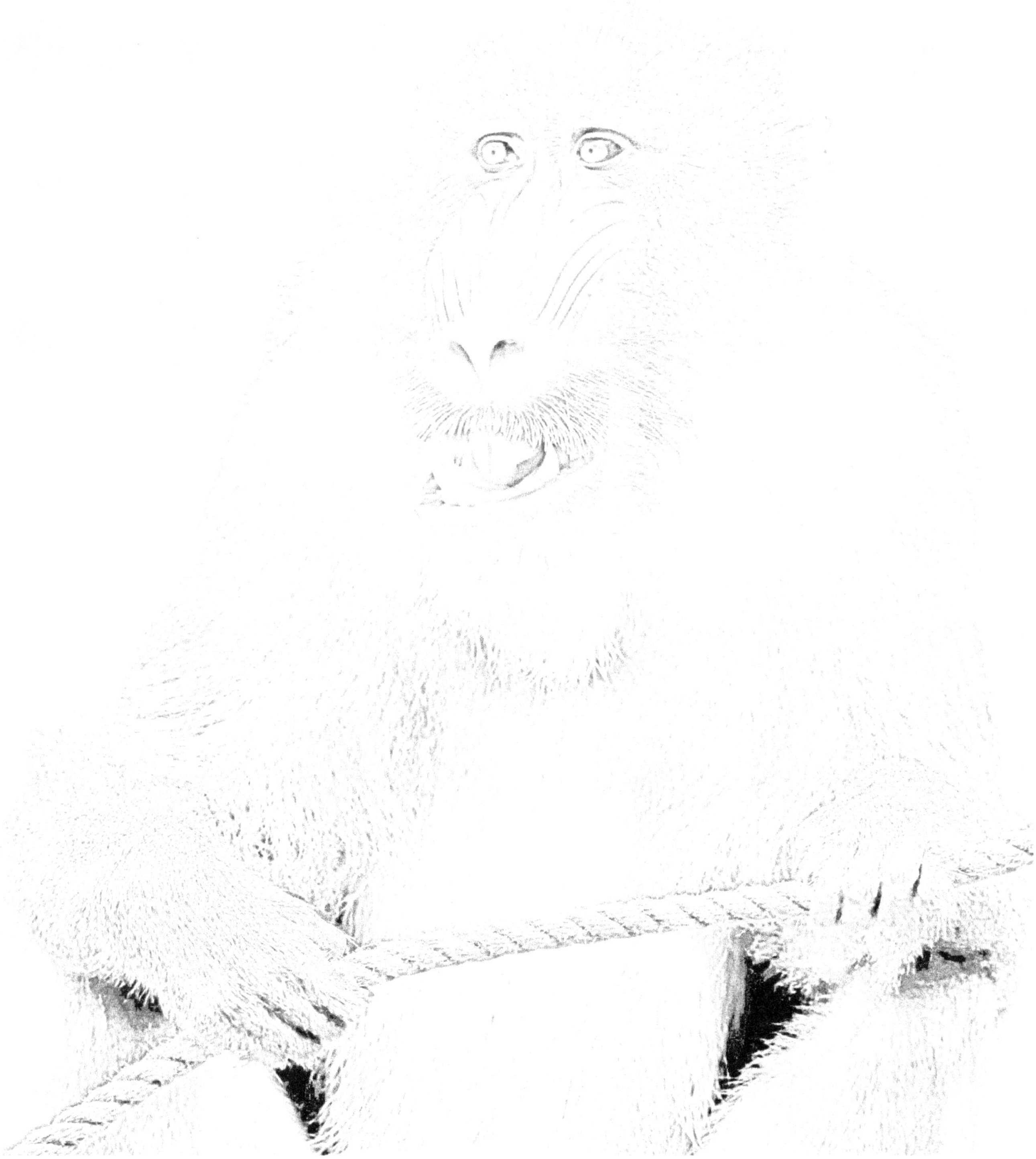

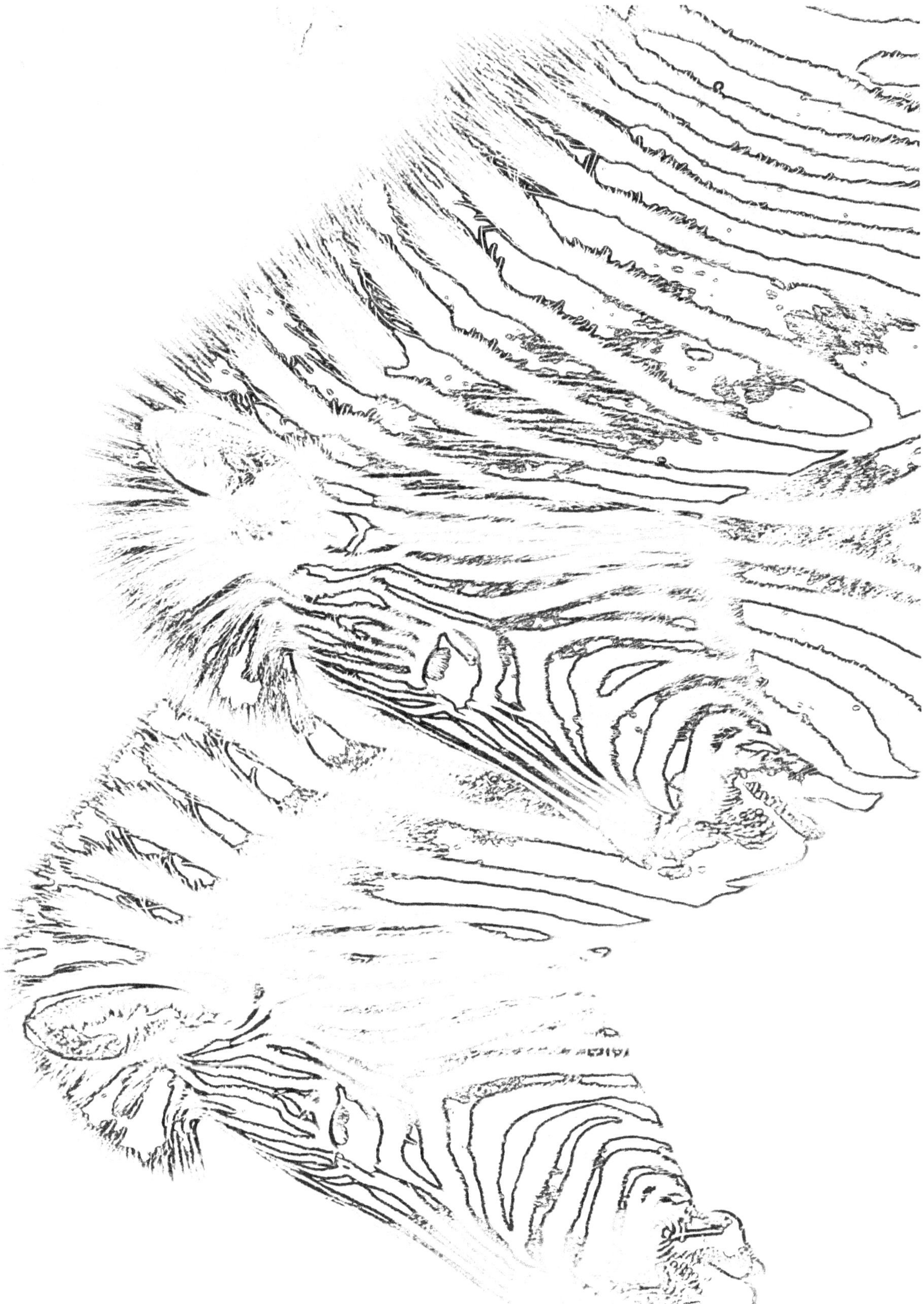

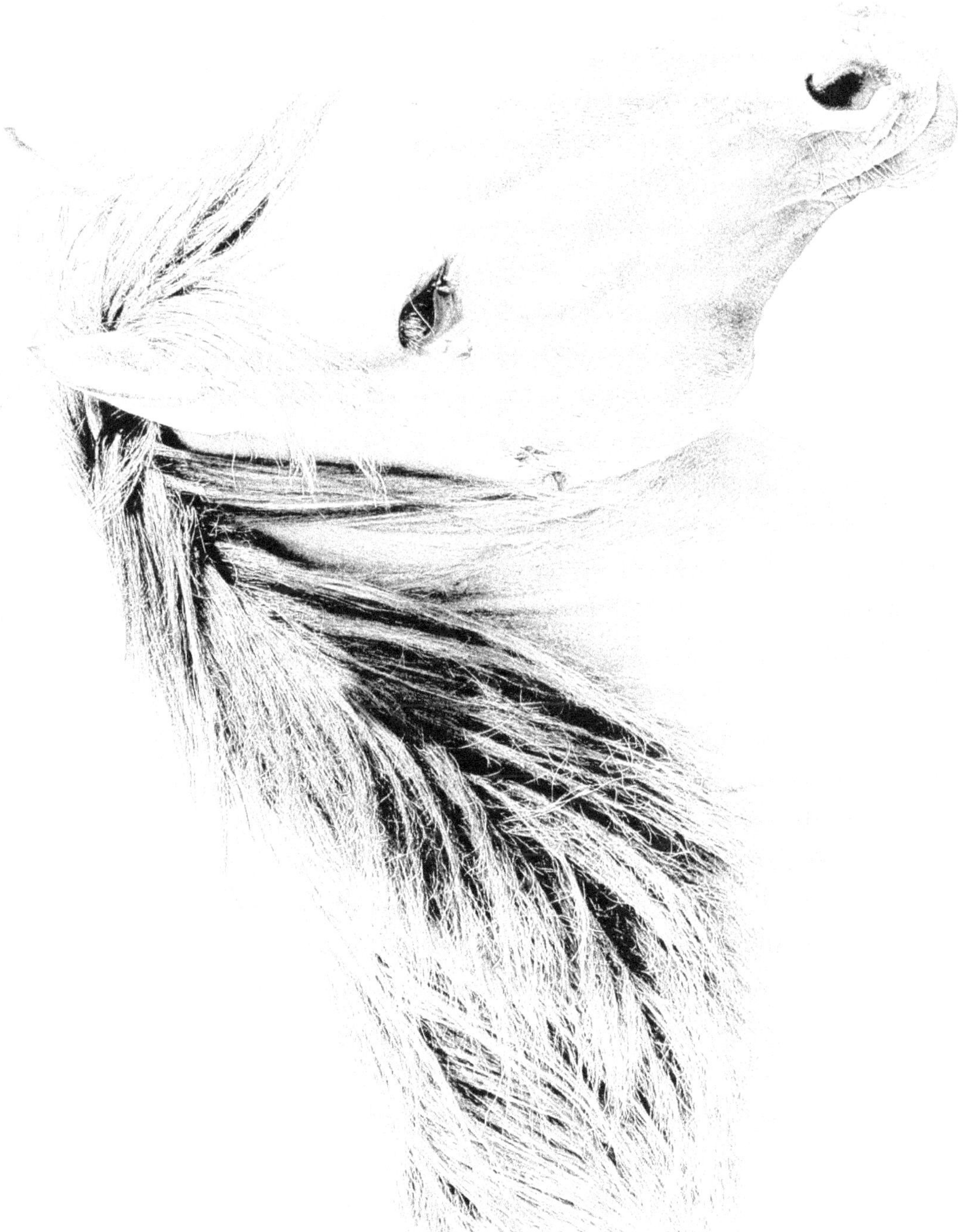

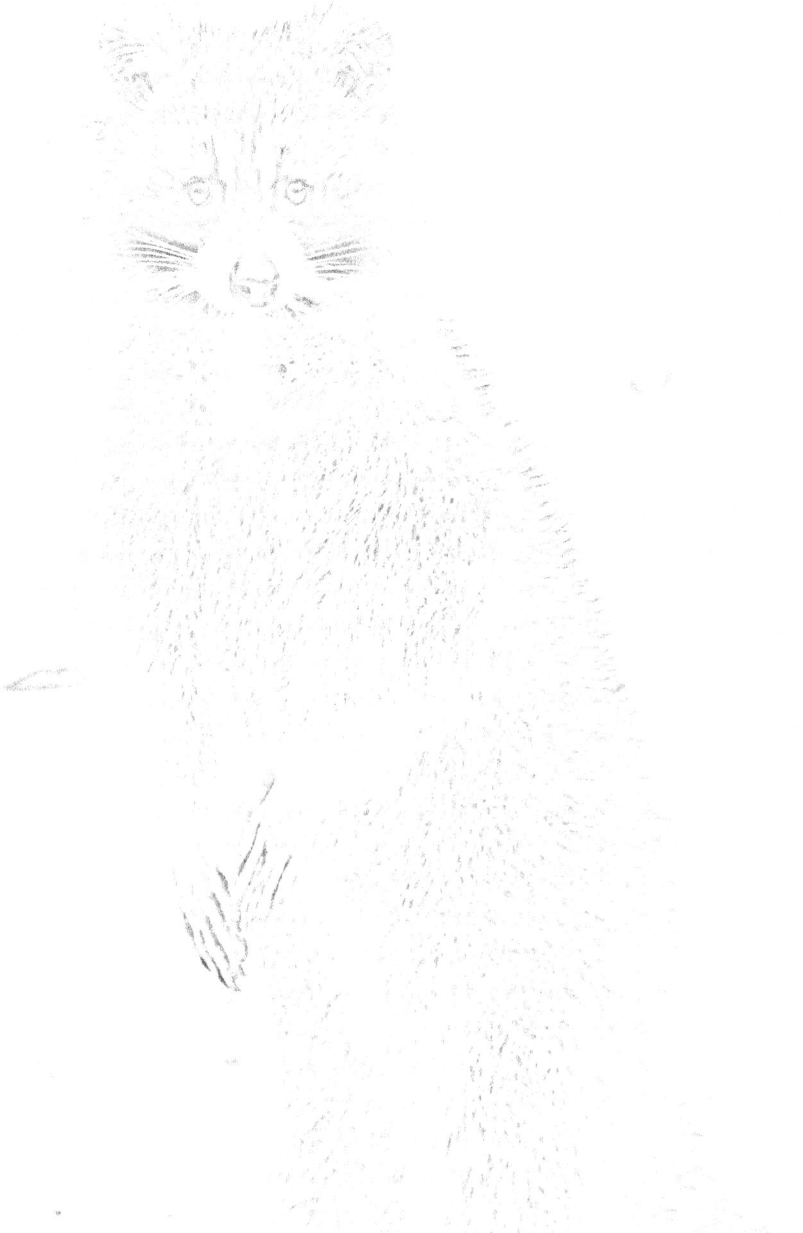

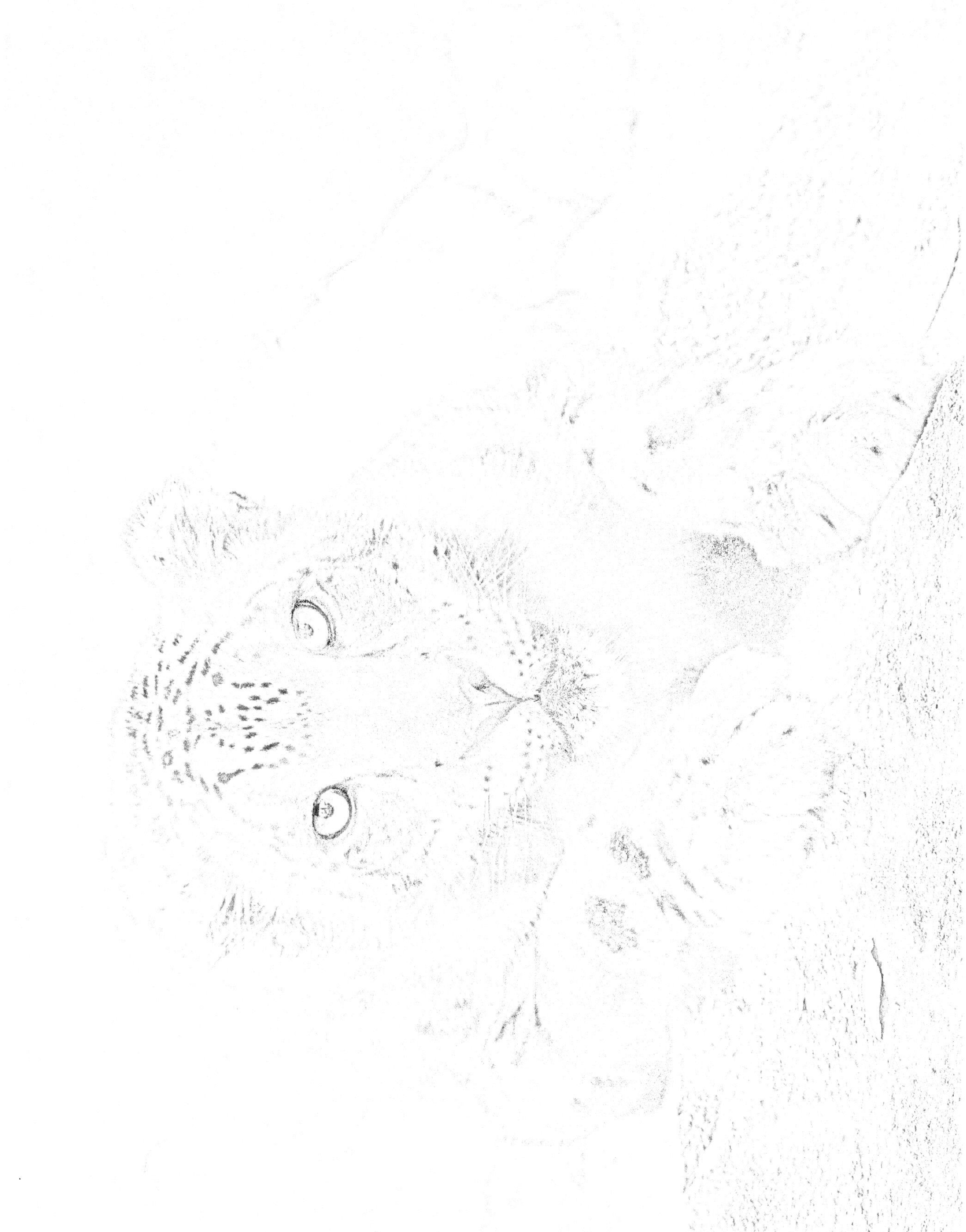

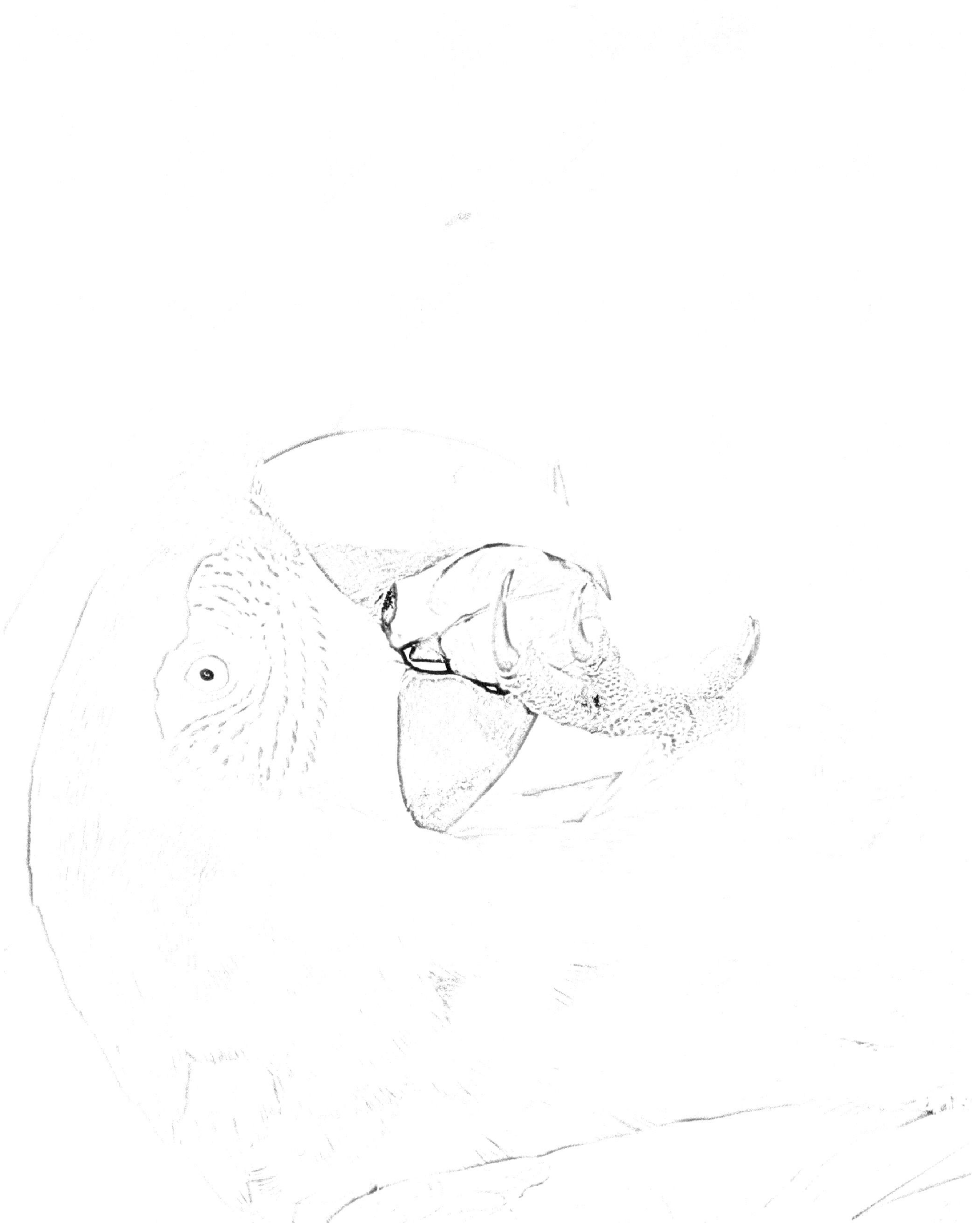

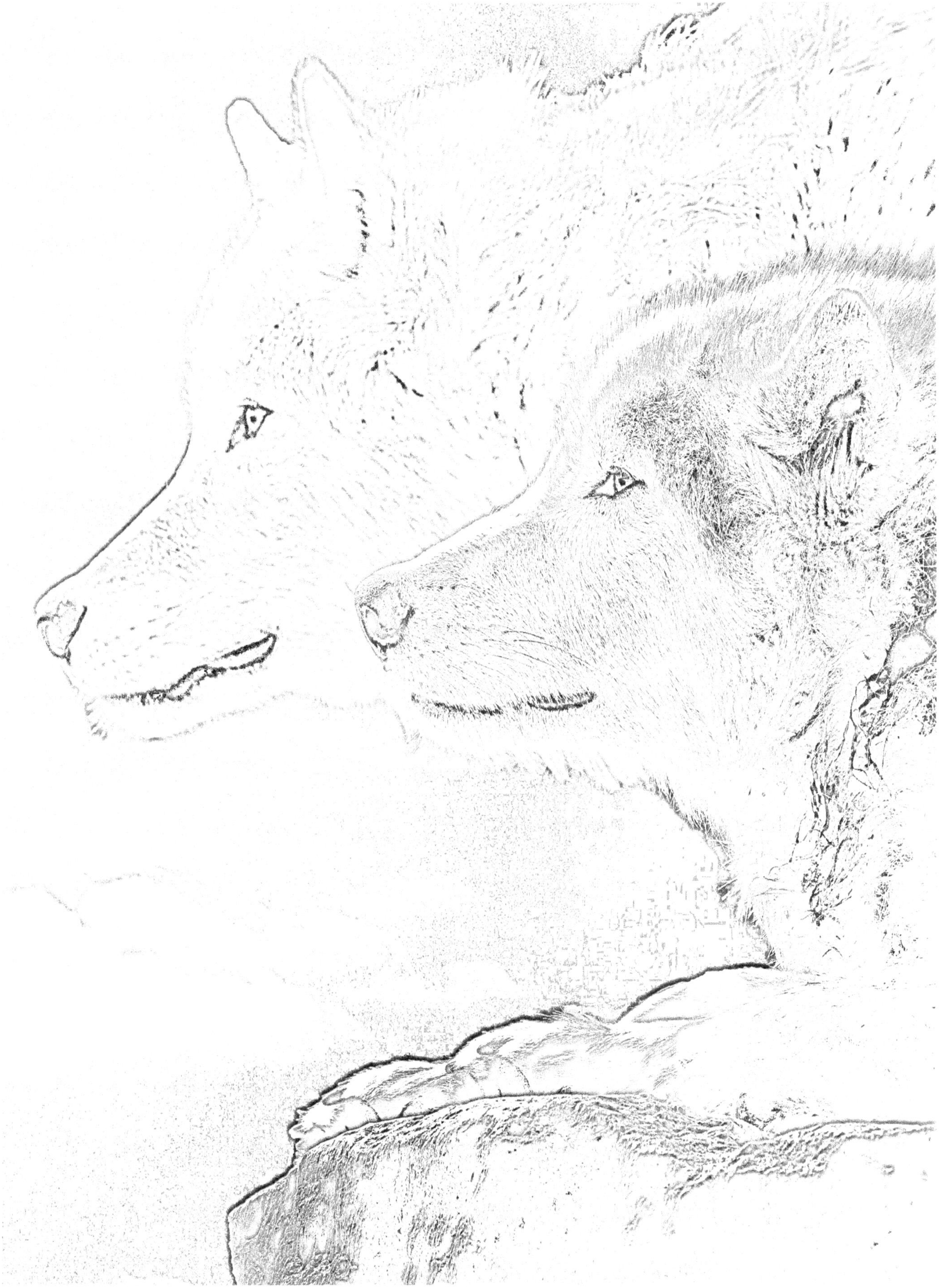

Thank you for ordering our coloring book!

More coloring books coming soon!

Thanks again!

Don

www.ingramcontent.com/pod-product-compliance
Lightning Source LLC
Chambersburg PA
CBHW081257180526
45170CB00007B/2467
*9781542601108*